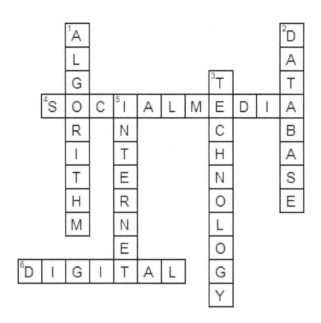

DIGITAL, INTERNET AND SOCIAL MEDIA

CROSSWORD PUZZLES

Volume I (2nd EDITION)

DINESH AGARAM

1

About the Author

Dinesh Agaram is a word-play enthusiast, and holds advanced degrees in mathematics, computer science and management. He has donned several professional hats in a twenty-year career in the corporate world, most recently as a consultant working at the intersection of behaviour, technology and change. Dinesh lives in Langley, United Kingdom.

PREFACE

I have always been fascinated with words and desired to create something new for wide consumption based on word-play. Thus, this series of crossword puzzle books. The idea for the theme, though, emerged from my interest and experience constructing topical crosswords as a student at university.

Solving a crossword puzzle is a discerning way to indulge one's interest in words. This volume of the series offers twenty-one such puzzles, all based on terminology picked from the Digital, Internet, Social Media, Online Marketing and Information Technology world.

The puzzles here are of varying levels of difficulty, and targeted for consumption of the interested student or professional working in the areas under the theme – although, anyone that has a love for technology and its manifestations in the present world and is an avid user of the internet and social media will very likely be able to successfully answer most of the clues.

Good luck solving them all!

Dinesh Agaram

ACKNOWLEDGEMENTS

TVK, your suggestions on cover design were valuable; your enthusiasm for trying out samples from the book encouraged me to focus and complete it.

Elmira, you have given me very valuable suggestions on cover design and content and have challenged me with the right questions about production quality.

Sai, your suggestions on crossword convention and making clues more interesting have been on point; I have incorporated them all.

Medina, your enthusiasm for the project through reviewing of sample puzzles, and your sustained encouragement to me to complete the project – these have been invaluable.

Ranga, your encouragement and support has been immense as always and a source of strength on this (and every) project of mine.

My sincere thanks to all of you, and to the others that have contributed to this series of crossword puzzle books in so many little useful ways.

Contents

WARM-UP

A section with three simple(r) puzzles, designed to get you into the groove. Dig into your memory for words such as those that begin with A, B, C, D, … I am not going to give away the words, am I?

Get going without wasting time! Remember though, that this section has words from every possible topic in the book's theme.

WARM-UP 1

Across

6. symbol representing number or letter (9)
7. Copy made incase original is lost (6)
8. very big integrated software for business (3) (abbrev.)
9. one cycle per second frequency (5)

Down

1. high-level tongue for scientific calculations (7)
2. two power thirty bytes (8)
3. background request handling process (6)
4. Adobe's change-me-not reader (7)
5. Jobs' my-talker device (6)

WARM-UP 2

Across

5. a string of characters to gain access (8)
6. line-up one behind the other (5)
7. device forwards data packets in network (6)
8. computer out of a full-length coat (3)
9. concurrent class-based coffee tongue (4)

Down

1. one press on the symbol board (9)
2. get in at the end, get out before everyone (4) (abbrev.)
3. set the device on fire (6)
4. freely used, shared and built-on information [4,4]

WARM-UP 3

Across

2. upload video to share here (7)
4. setting a new business in motion [5-2]
8. results order could be based on this google value (8)
9. restart via the OS when already on (4,4)
10. set off this procedural database code (7)

Down

1. microsoft's scripting tongue (8)
3. fastening up the files together at high speed (7)
5. raise to a higher standard (7)
6. cuts into computers unauthorised (6)
7. meta-tongue for customised markups (3) (abbrev.)

ALL ABOUT DATA

Most of the big inventions of the early years of Information Technology related to data and data processing. The two puzzles in this section attempt to entertain you by bringing to you terms from that era, as well as those coined newly in this millennium. They will test your abilities and memory in deciphering terms that you have perhaps used one time or the other during your involvement with systems, information processing and wrangling of data.

ALL ABOUT DATA 1

Across

1. this information is available for everyone to access (4,4)
6. 10-powered byte (8)
8. pose this sequence well in the collection (5)
9. use this principally to unlock whole rows of table information (7,3)
10. this unique thing to spot an entity such as a document or record (4) (abbrev.)
11. graphically ask through exemplification (5,2,7)
12. don at a till area full of tables (10,4)
14. compressing to take less space in storage (7)
15. use this elevated small font for the footnote (11)

Down

2. this part of the data is non-redundant, non-compressible. measure it! (7)
3. auto-pull this stored procedure when database event occurs (7)
4. the dbms's efficiency driver for the things you pose to it (5,9)
5. just about the information you have (8)
7. check this unnecessary repetition in two or more tables (10)
13. throw a big one into the columns (3) (acron.)

ALL ABOUT DATA 2

Across

3. Is a method to manipulate indexes for fast retrieval (4) (abbrev.)
4. the inventory for installed IT assets and their relationships (4)(abbrev.)
8. computer generated data is a result of some operations (6)
9. this nonrelational storer doesnt continue the story (5)
10. the wise female high priest of databases (6)
13. window to ask questions, receive information (5,9)
15. identify element in the array using small font just below line (9)
16. send this across the network, one block in transmission (6)

Down

1. the top guy in stack gets out before everyone else, as a consolation (4) (acron.)
2. is worried about how data will be stored, consumed, integrated and managed by different data entities and IT systems (4,9)
5. COM-based architectural reusability middleman (4) (abbrev.)
6. go stand at the back of the line to do IPC content transfer (7,5)
7. it's got no value, but it does not have a zero. However, a false on the boolean test (4,8)
11. with this, the file uses less space when stored (11)
12. the name establishes the object - physical or otherwise (10)
14. LX powered memory size (7)

SUPER JUMBLE 1 (EASY)

The super jumbles are puzzles that combine a range of topics and test your all-round ability with terms in digital, social media and technology - including *hardware*, *software* and *engineering*.

This first super jumble is meant for casual play and does not require flexing your neural circuitry to its edges.

SUPER JUMBLE EASY!

Across

3. the perpetual beep sounds come from transaction systems here in retail (5,2,4)
4. outer equipment (10)
6. click leads to drop, reveals variety to choose from (4-4,4)
11. maternal printed slotter for computer components (11)
12. a revived corpse controlled without its knowledge and used for sending spam or illicit stuff (6)
13. oblique slant or progressive slit (7,5)
14. town east of Rome is brand at IBM's service (6)

Down

1. smallest addressable physical point in this raster (5)
2. holds shortcuts to launch when starting Windows (7,6)
5. traversing the entirety, a full addressing of the problem (3-2-3)
7. erase and reprogram, but can only read from it (6) [abbrev.]
8. printed version of the document (4,4)
9. this customer is capable of obtaining information and applications from a server (6)
10. tough storage device has a magnetic core (4,4)

THE INTERNET

Can you imagine a world without the internet? Can you imagine not being *online* for a single waking hour, let alone a single day?

The early work on this behind-the-scenes information super-highway of the world began in the 1960s. Bring the focus to today, and it has been the reason for the birth of hundreds of new terms – in essence, a whole new vocabulary. These words have become mainstay in our tongues, subordinating age-old ones with an undefeatable force and speed.

Try these out and you will not be disappointed - after all, these are the terms you have been using and debating about every day!

Crack on, go *offline* to solve these!

THE INTERNET 1

Across

2. noisy and violent internet portal with search (5)
4. even with fifty, these programs are libre (4) (abbrev.)
8. show keenness to discover content on www (9)
11. this has personal relation lines of internet users (6,5)
13. this one instance of a visit to the web leaf (4,4)
14. information, identification label (3)

Down

1. Cad stops tuning into digital audio on Net (8)
2. carpe diem for youth on social media (4) (acron.)
3. while not directly connected to the Net (7)
5. this site brings together information from diverse sources, gives access to all of them (3,6)
6. web application in the native browser (6,3)
7. so you can identify each device on the network (2,7)
9. altruistic program dishes out internet pages over hypertext (3,6)
10. cuts into without authorization (6)
12. hah! stag makes it easier to spot the theme (7)

THE INTERNET 2

Across

1. anchor gateway site giving access to a range of services and functions (6)
8. these use real-time geo-data from device to offer information and entertainment (8-5,8)
10. linking through the neighbouring smart chap to the world (9)
11. the work's not protected by copyright (6,6)
12. outlook's a sizzling post company sending your web communication to another (7)
13. smooth browser, credited to be amongst the first for the Net to be widely distributed (6)
14. its only decent to follow these propriety rules virtually (10)
15. google this procedure; considers number and importance of inbound links as significant (8)

Down

2. valid credential for a single login (3,4,8)
3. Internet standard that extends the format of email to support non-ASCII, multiple media (4) (abbrev.)
4. make electronic transactions from this purse (7,6)
5. an individual's custom web link (8,3)
6. unmisanthropic mingling web place for many people, a literary countenance (8)
7. shared video on google site by upload (7)
8. know and professionally trust my people in this web place (8)
9. the short automated program running over the Net (3)

THE INTERNET 3

Across

1. this online curler only consumes, doesnt participate (6)
7. you'd usually land in this front room first on the web (4,4)
8. upload photos and short videos on your mobile here... come on, network socially (9)
9. use net forum to discuss particular topics (9)
10. Terra's better searcher half from 2000 (5)
11. broadcasting smaller content (13)
12. software to move email using client-server architecture (4,8,5)
14. commercial's marketing not distinct from subject content, on website (6,11)

Down

2. marketing is for evenly increasing this number on websites (8)
3. gather and disperse, perform publicly inbetween (5,3)
4. XML, HTTP, SMTP, all in this one, to exchange info between web services... a protocol (4) (abbrev.)
5. cant allow a higher rate of cell transfer along network (4,4,4)
6. a little soapy interoperable functionality (3,7)
11. image, video, et al. spread rapidly through forwards, maybe with some variation (4)
13. guarantee you are one of its kind universally (4) (abbrev.)

SUPER JUMBLE 2 (DIFFICULT)

The super jumbles are designed to test your all-round grasp and recollection of terms. In this volume, they have been picked specifically for coverage - you may find the answer to a clue lies in artificial intelligence and find the next to be about object orientation. And yet, the next one may be about a general concept in IT operations! Wait a minute, am I revealing too much, already?

Go in with a spirit of challenge, and you will not be disappointed!

THE SUPER JUMBLE 2

Across

3. in this breach, the attacker pretends to be authorized to gain access or greater privilege (10)
5. a local program for a local platform (6,3)
7. std. poke the computer in its area (7)
12. induced brilliance when voltage is applied (3) (abbrev.)
13. this space is made accessible to multiple network users (6,9)
14. a flamboyant drive to remember (6,5)
15. african bird's eye chilli, wild outer equipment that connects to your main one (10)
16. a few initial instructions to load a program, without external help or capital (13)
17. system of connections that makes block data storage appear locally attached (7,4,7)

Down

1. foes made, now diagnosing will help fix (4,4)
2. almost none of the wriggly stuff connecting devices (8)
4. 'cos it sounds like users are watching this measurement of performance (7,2,7)
6. the actual message in transmitted data, not headers, not description of it (7)
8. the basic structure underlying a concept or system (9)
9. s/he belongs to the www, whether naturalised or not (7)
10. many ways of communicating (10)
11. your ideal customer's fictional representation (4,7)

23

ALGORITHMS

Realising benefits out of Information Technology commenced with algorithms. They provide the structure to code. The puzzles in the section will take you into a brass-tacks world where you will recollect experiences of learning the methods that formed the basis of much of the nice magic of technology that we get to use in our daily lives.

Go on, take a stab at these!

ALGORITHMS 1

Across

3. samely executable everywhere, no recompiling (6,10)
5. this string's got fixed meaning, cant redefine (8,4)
6. leave that bit in transmission to detect errors (6)
8. this thing has atleast one that's pure, virtual, and can only be used fundamentally... usually at the top (8,4,5)
9. they are complete in themselves, not fractions (8)

Down

1. cant blame the group for its compressed image (4) (abbrev.)
2. relating to its product and of all integers below it (9)
4. hurriedly arrange in order (5,4)
7. a pile of things, either a hierarchy of software layers or just data as it comes (5)

ALGORITHMS 2

Across

4. exactly describe context-free grammars using this notation (6-4,4)
5. Tim in HR goal to follow calculation process (9)
7. an algorithm that can exhibit different behaviors on different runs (3-13)
10. operating on whole arrays or converting a matrix into a column (13)

Down

1. defined in terms of itself (9)
2. a way to represent a variety of information symbols (9,8)
3. working simultaneously, could be at bit-level, instruction-level or task-level (15)
6. add up previous lies in this unique sequence pattern (9)
8. give away this result of computation (6)
9. throw in this stuff to be processed (5)
11. an enhanced way to express grammar of a formal language (4) (abbrev.)

ALGORITHMS 3

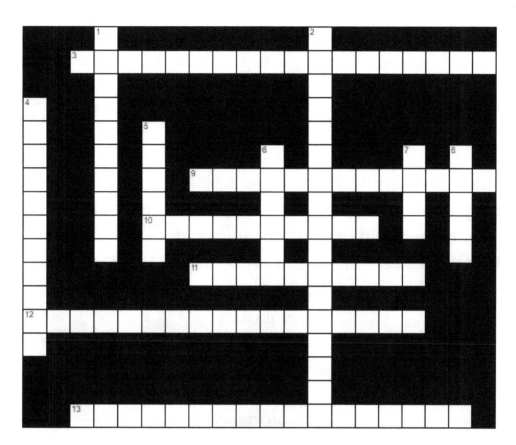

Across

3. mathematical model that can be in exactly one of a bounded number of states (6,5,7)
9. you may be asked to get into line here, but you would still pull your weight (8,5)
10. truest ting on the machine's ability to think (6,4)
11. quantitatively true member (4,6)
12. this thing has atleast one that's pure, virtual, and can only be used fundamentally... usually at the top (8,4,5)
13. number based approximation methods for solving problems (9,8)

Down

1. structurally fit to carry at most two children at every node (6,4)
2. calling itself is in procedure (9,8)
4. four square symbols in this positional numeral system (11)
5. not data, but file to check its integrity, assist recovery (6)
6. go logo a century-powered number (6)
7. hypothesis is, it has no value (4)
8. The queen wouldn't have to stand in this structure (5)

SUPER JUMBLE 3 (MORE DIFFICULT)

Once more, a difficult super jumble. Assuming you have completed all the puzzles before this one, you have already warmed up and flexed your mental abilities sufficiently to attempt this super difficult grid. It combines very interesting terms that evolved in the 100 years' plus history of the tech field, including the latest terms in its vocabulary.

Crack this, and you are set to complete this volume of puzzles comfortably!

A SUPER DIFFICULT JUMBLE

Across

5. document christened with an extension (4,4)
6. following the instruction, delay before data transfer begins (7)
8. words adjusted to margins and spacing, fully justified (4,9)
11. war meal software to disrupt and damage (7)
13. roles interact with systems through this to achieve goals (3,4)
15. a representation system, a first-order logic frame-based tongue, a reasoner, all (9,7)
16. an element of check on data makes it evenly binary (6,3)

Down

1. one formal and structured way of defining the enterprise (7,9)
2. touchy about being treated differently for capital and lower (4,9)
3. this investor loves small tech for expansion (7,10)
4. this pond of things is initialized, ready to use (6,4)
7. the tech lasts this duration in operation (4) (abbrev.)
9. contains all security credentials for a login session (6,5)
10. devices in chains within a building (3) (abbrev.)
12. skilled operator packs a punch (5,4)
14. feted device carrying current along channel with controllable resistance (3) (abbrev.)

PROGRAMMING

The most practically useful of terminology, used every day by coders around the world (some that have become somewhat obsolete even, except for use in crossword puzzles!) have been assembled into this set of grids. This will bring a smile to the faces of ones that love hitting up lines in different languages on their code editors.

Take a break from your intense work sessions and try these out!

PROGRAMMING 1

Across

2. gather to talk in a primitive tongue (8,8)
5. point in the clock when an association occurs (7,4)
6. lines with no effect on program output whatsoever (9,4)
9. prompt user in a small closed area for conversation (6,3)
10. imperative tongue suited to numeric and scientific computing (7)
13. a clear case of imitating by the program or device (9)
15. take a changing object, turn into object (4,1,8)
17. Oh oh! system modelled as a set of things which can be controlled and manipulated modularly (6-8)
18. a class of elements, each christened uniquely for that class, but could be shared with those in other classes (9)
19. can copy itself, corrupt and destroy (5)

Down

1. the argument, you see, is implicit, to the point (4,2,9)
3. the rules for combining symbols in the language (6)
4. the IDE for a fast fundamental language (6)
7. performs a one way transfer of control to another line (4)
8. disciplined type of usual language with speech defect (6,4)
11. LALR parser generator based on grammar similar to BNF. yeah! its a carbon copy (4) (acron.)
12. Java's ward is lightweight way of data interchange (4) (abbrev.)
14. many instances of this exalted type (5)
16. language that the lover of shoe-ties speaks in (3)

PROGRAMMING 2

Across

1. continue the story of requesting information from the database (3) (abbrev.)
4. coding for hardware (7,11)
7. the chap assists in detecting and correcting errors in programs (8)
8. software to update, fix, improve status quo (5)
9. this individual analyses and designs software for user effectiveness (6,7)
10. combining selection, sequence and loop, birds embed document in another (7)
11. a bookshelf collection full of reusable resources (7)
14. you see, uses this to pass actuals into function (4,2,5)
15. set of independent lines within a larger program, its a chore (7)

Down

1. checking if the letter strands are the same (6,10)
2. mathematical study of the meaning of the tongue, it's philosophy (9)
3. tongue evolved through use and repetition, no planning, no premeditation (7,8)
5. 00 insect could have followed 99 and created havoc around the millenium's turn (3) (abbrev.)
6. you could use this object-oriented bunch to develop desktop applications for a kind of ventilation (3) (abbrev.)
8. stays high-level, a non-venomous tongue (6)
12. tongue to describe units of work to OS/390 (3) (abbrev.)
13. architectural pattern to separate representation from presentation, enables reuse (3) (abbrev.)

PROGRAMMING 3

Across

1. single endpoint comms channel, can test one's own network (8)
2. a framework on which applications may be run (8)
5. member of parliament goes to los angeles, or vice versa, for this bundled web development platform (4) (abbrev.)
6. principle that takes future growth into consideration, a measure of that ability (13)
8. make that code change in a small area (5)
11. compiler's creator converting intermediate to executable, all by itself (4,10)
13. this IDE from NXP only supports assembly, C & C++ (11)
14. features practice that's superseded, as it's no longer efficient; backwardly kind, though (11)
15. numbers that like to be by themselves (8)

Down

1. replace and compile, transform while improving performance with a do, while you do (4,9)
3. today's malicious email catch will include some individuals' credit card and password information (8)
4. the source is this long, measured in its thousands (4)
7. free the lines to study, change and distribute (4,6)
9. options appear on the right-click (3-2,4)
10. indonesian isle's reusable seeds are serializable, go get and set them (9)
12. you are doing this when writing, testing & debugging computer programs (6)
13. Microsoft's binary interface standard of 1993 (3) (abbrev.)

TOOLS N TECH

Technology means not just software. It also means devices and implements that can held in the hand, spoken into, spoken to, and carried around. This set of puzzles will give problem-solvers a chance to look around them and see if more clues can be found in the electronic things they possess.

Try these with confidence! If you get stuck, yes, look around yourself for the answers!

TOOLS N TECH 1

Across

1. object relational mapping during a long deep sleep (9)
4. er... milk for ape is not just relational db, not just application over it, is also cross-platform (9,3)
9. capable of performing even when connected devices have different operators and manufacturers (8-11)
11. wear helmet, interact with these 3d images (7,7)
13. service to listen and identify music from the island country (6)
14. the sensation of participating in distant events (12)
15. strictly for social networking within organisations, it's freemium (6)

Down

2. how dare you record and edit multiple tracks with this! (8)
3. store, manipulate, format text using this (4,9)
4. satellite communication channel access method gives users one or several frequency bands (4) (abbrev.)
5. chap's used all by itself without connection to network (5-5)
6. small enough to carry (8)
7. could be a small gadget, or a part of user middleman to perform function or access service (6)
8. set this portable reader on fire (6)
10. one that ultimately handles the product (3,4)
12. listen and talk, you are the eye of the apple (6)

TOOLS N TECH 2

Across

1. standard layout on English-language typewriters and keyboards (6)
4. e-scuba tool to make, mix and master the ears (6)
6. on sleep mode for too long, conserving power (7)
8. low level Windows' APIs for high-performance multimedia support (7)
11. iconic pointer to data or program (8)
12. use type of statistics to say future trends, behaviour (10,9)
13. Borland's hollow IDE is a structured communication technique from ancient Greece (6)
15. horizontal one, below title at the top, drops down, gives you choices (4,3)
16. not open, privately owned, controlled (11)
17. part of the product directly accessed by user, that allows access to more (5-3)

Down

2. writer mimicking appearance of ordinary ink (10,5)
3. begin here for access to Windows' computer programs (5,6)
5. bunch of architectural principles to integrate enterprise computer applications (3) (abbrev.)
7. this one opens windows to show programs and processes running (4,7)
9. massaging the mouse on the other side makes it drop down (5,5)
10. the thin medium's not more than a few inches square, but has got a magnetic personality (6,4)
14. component enabling additive customisation (4-2)

TOOLS N TECH 3

Across

2. measured amount of data a persister can hold (7, 8)
5. superior-inferior model of unidirectional control amongst devices (6-5)
7. chap religiously forwards data packets to the right places in network (6)
8. the benevolent chap in the corner sending and receiving email (4,6)
9. IC with logic blocks can be configured using HDL (4) (abbrev.)
10. the rule of yearly doubling of transistors per square inch (6,3)
14. Adobe's rapid platform and language (10)
15. use this to capture handwriting and drawing on your device's UI (7,3)
16. solar release in 1999 of Javan page creating technology (3) (abbrev.)

Down

1. catholic one-at-a-time transport connects devices to controller (3) (abbrev.)
3. Rep's plea turn mooc device into a design for use by one individual at a time (8,8)
4. a panel of strikables to operate your desktop (8)
6. ADOBE'S CHANGE-ME-NOT READER (7)
11. sit, slap, topple and cuddle this portable computer (6)
12. its a connection point to travel through, crossing device boundaries (4)
13. with this tech standard, devices, computers and electronic crooners can talk to each other (4) (acron.)

SUPER JUMBLE 4 (MIXED)

We have come to the last puzzle in this volume of crossword puzzles. Sharpen your pencil and embark on these. They may or may not tax your brain much, but that doesn't matter. Having surmounted the most difficult of puzzles, you now deserve a bit of relaxation.

Hang on… not all the clues in this jumble are that easy! Don't you want to feel like you have accomplished something when you finish?

Thank you again for enjoying this book!

A SUPER MIXED JUMBLE

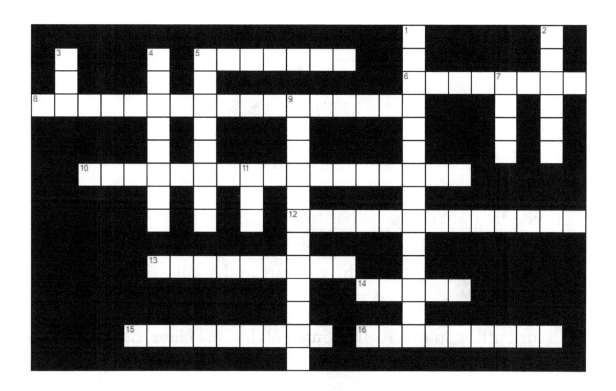

Across

5. run untested software here securely, virtually with silica inside (7)
6. font family with common design features (8)
8. device for displaying input signals as characters on a screen (6,7,4)
10. engineering to separate presentation, application processing and data management (1-4, 12)
12. flowing display with oriented molecules (8,7)
13. every pixel in this image is of intensity (9)
14. nimble, short phases, move quickly, frequent adaptions... way to develop (5)
15. indecision in adding white noise to reduce distortion (9)
16. running programs to assess performance characteristics, perhaps using standard tests and trials (9)

Down

1. piecing together systems from below to the top (6-2,6)
2. nothing destructive about Barry's estimation model for software (6) (abbrev.)
3. this middleman allows users to interact with the hard ones in a user friendly manner (3) (abbrev.)
4. mine fuel for this first item in the choice bar (4,4)
5. visual element distinguishing distribution of responsibility within business processes (8)
7. size, pitch, spacing, typeface, all are part of this design choice (4)
9. an initial gas release will straighten the lines (12)
11. 5-level evolutionary standard to mature software development (3) (abbrev.)

SOLUTIONS

Lest you thought this page had any solutions, let me clarify that as author, I am incredibly pleased you have attempted the puzzles and welcome you to check the answers in the following pages.

If you have reached here due to an urge to look up the answers without putting in much effort into solving the clues, do not give in to the temptation! Go back to the puzzle page, take a fresh stab - with a fresh mind - after a cup of coffee perhaps. Allow yourself to have as much fun as you can – the pleasure will be the author's, too!

WARM-UP 1

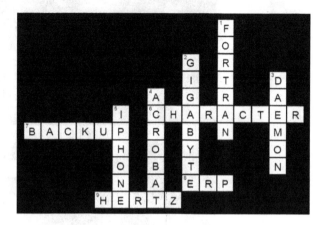

WARM-UP 2

WARM-UP 3

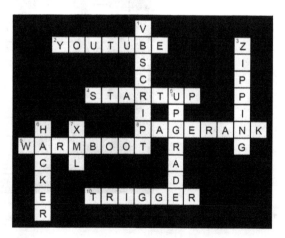

ALL ABOUT DATA 1

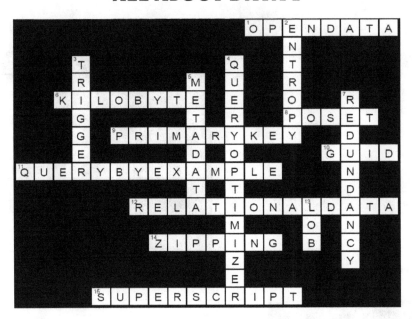

ALL ABOUT DATA 2

SUPER JUMBLE 1

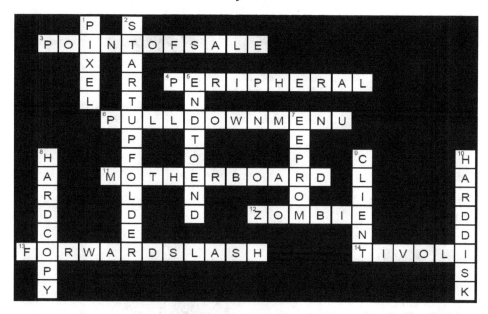

THE INTERNET 1

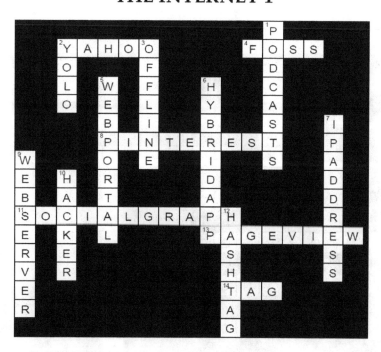

THE INTERNET 2

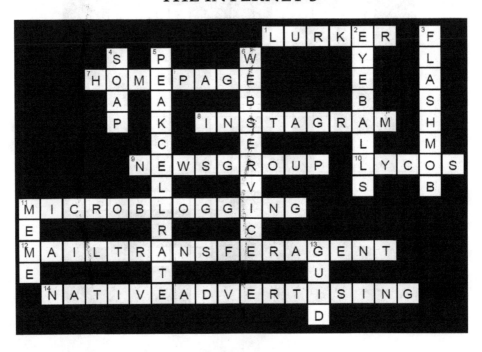

THE INTERNET 3

SUPER JUMBLE 2

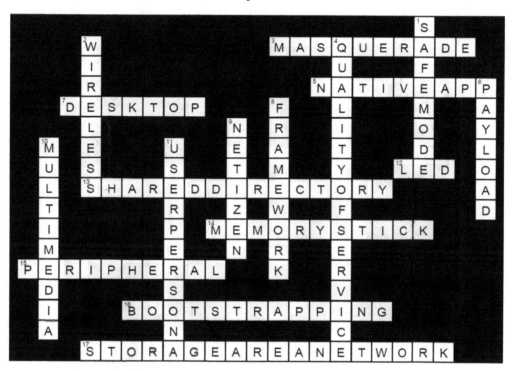

ALGORITHMS 1

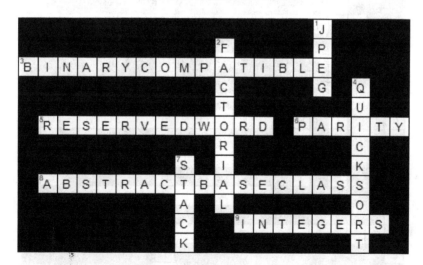

ALGORITHMS 2

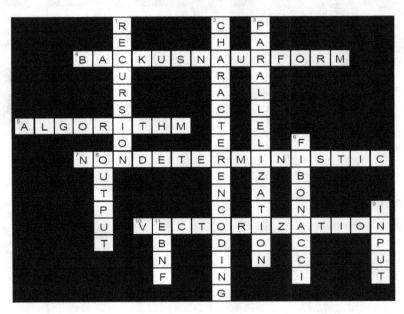

ALGORITHMS 3

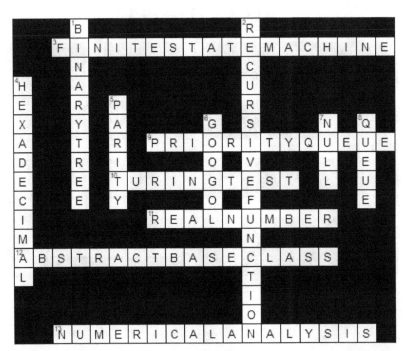

SUPER JUMBLE 3

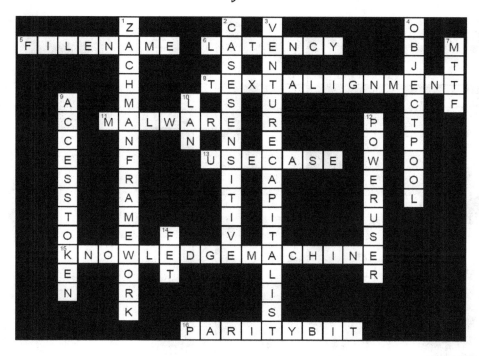

PROGRAMMING 1

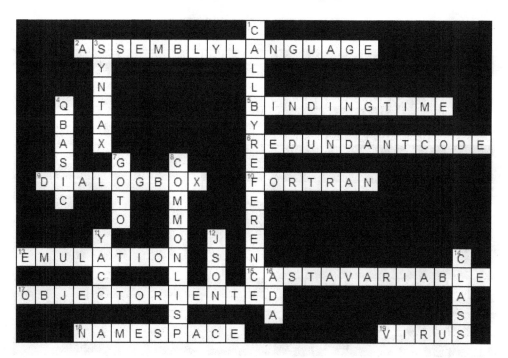

PROGRAMMING 2

PROGRAMMING 3

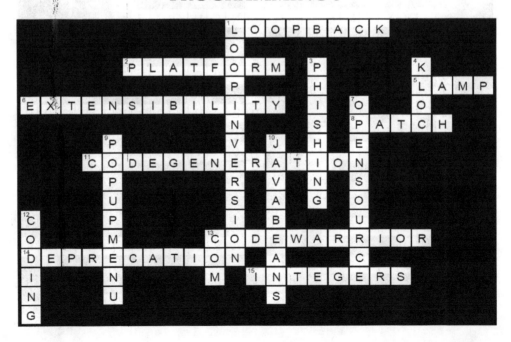

TOOLS N TECH 1

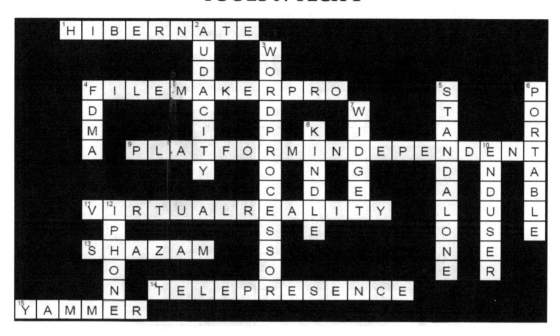

TOOLS N TECH 2

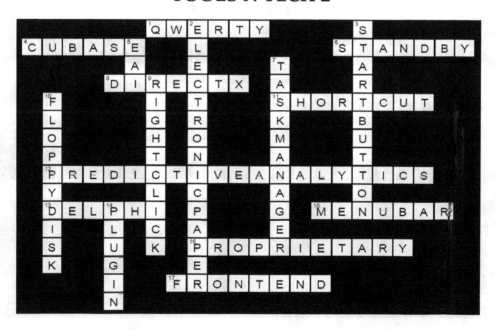

TOOLS N TECH 3

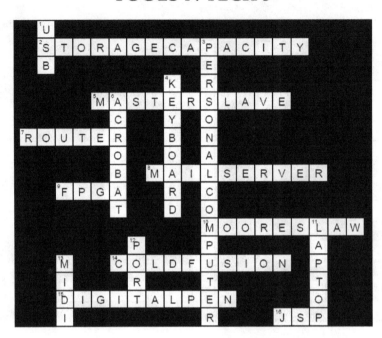

SUPER JUMBLE 4

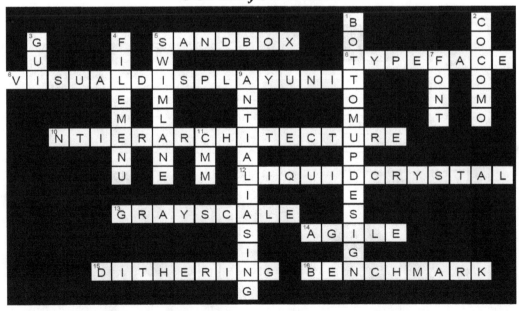

www.ingramcontent.com/pod-product-compliance
Lightning Source LLC
Chambersburg PA
CBHW080605060326
40689CB00021B/4938